THE SERVICE BUSINESS WAR MANUAL

From the Trenches to a Multi-Million Dollar Operation

RONALD OSBORNE
Award-Winning International Business Coach

Published by Ronald Osborne

ISBN: 978-1-7645151-0-8 (Paperback)
ISBN: 978-1-7645151-1-5 (eBook)

CONTENTS

INTRODUCTION

The War for Service Dominance

If you open social media right now, you will see a lot of noise. You'll see 20-year-olds renting Lamborghinis telling you that you can make millions by working four hours a week, or that you can get rich quick by dropshipping products you've never touched.

Let's call that what it is: BS.

If you run a service business—if you are a roofer, a chiropractor, an electrician, or an accountant—you know that business isn't built on hacks or manifestation. It is built on sweat, logistics, and dealing with real human beings who are often unhappy until you fix their problem.

I wrote this book because I want to offer you something real.

I am not a guru who made money teaching people how to make money. I am a businessman who learned discipline the hard way. My management experience didn't come from a textbook; it came from serving in the Australian Army and from building my own companies from scratch.

When I left the military due to a medical discharge—an injury to my stomach that still affects me today—I didn't look for a handout. I built my first company, TWECS (Telecommunications Wireless Electrical Civil Construction Solutions), from the ground up. I took that company from a chaotic startup to a machine generating $5.7 million in revenue with 30 employees operating up and down the east coast of Australia.

I have built construction companies, digital marketing agencies, and roofing businesses. I have hired family, I have fired friends, and I have the scars to prove it. I have an MBA specializing in finance, but I don't speak in academic theories. I speak in numbers, sweat, and profit.

The Free Value Philosophy

You might be wondering, Ronald, if you know so much, why aren't you charging $5,000 for this information?

Here is the honest truth: I believe in leading with value. If you go to my website right now, you will find marketing ROI calculators, cash flow templates, contractor quote generators, and Reddit scrapers—all for free.

Why? Because charging $197 a month for a tool that costs me $4 to run is, in my eyes, haram. I believe that if I help you win, if I help you get that first leg up, you will remember who helped you when you're ready to scale to the millions. That is how you build a reputation. That is how you build a legacy.

The Reality of Business Failure

Let's look at the cold, hard facts. 90% of startups fail. Almost half of all businesses stop operating after five years.

Why do they fail? They don't fail because the owner didn't manifest enough success. They fail because of cash flow problems. They fail because they hired the wrong people. They fail because they spent $15,000 on Google Ads without knowing their numbers. They fail because they didn't have a plan.

This book is about moving you from Self-Employed Laborer to Business Owner. It is about stopping the guesswork. We are going to talk about the hard things. We are going to talk about validation, cash flow, and the loneliness of leadership.

We are going to cover everything from the soldier's mindset to the technicalities of SEO and lead generation. We are going to talk about hiring (and the $130,000 mistake I made hiring a friend). We are going to talk about automating your service business using AI agents so you can actually live your life.

Opportunity waits for no man. Let's get to work.

KEY TAKEAWAYS

✓ 90% of startups fail—most due to cash flow, not lack of passion

✓ This book moves you from Self-Employed Laborer to Business Owner

✓ Free tools and templates are available at ronaldosborne.org

✓ Success comes from systems, not hustle culture or manifestation

CHAPTER 1: The Operator's Mindset: Validation, Risk, and The Pipe Dream

People often ask me, Ronald, what was harder: serving in the Australian Army or building a business?

They expect me to say the Army. They expect me to say that the physical toll, the discipline, the sleeping in the mud, or the operations were the hardest things I've ever done. But I'll tell you the honest truth: I have had far more sleepless nights as a business owner than I ever did as a soldier.

In the Army, even when things are tough, you have a brotherhood. You have orders. You know exactly what you need to do. You are part of a machine that is bigger than you. In business, especially in the beginning, you are often alone in the dark, wondering if you're going to make payroll. You are the one who has to make the decision. If the decision is wrong, it's on you. If the client doesn't pay, it's on you. If the employee quits, it's on you.

Starting a business is one of the most difficult things I have ever done in my entire life. This chapter is about preparing your mind for that reality. Before we talk about SEO, cash flow, or hiring, we need to talk about Validation, Risk, and the Strategy of Focus.

The Pipe Dream vs. Reality

Everyone believes their business idea is the one that will make millions. If you didn't believe that, why would you wake up in the morning? But you need to bring yourself back down to earth. You need to validate your idea before you bet your life savings on it. I see people chasing what I call pipe dreams—ideas that have no basis in reality.

Case Study: The Travel App Pipe Dream

I once engaged with an individual looking for investors for a travel company. He was targeting international markets and looking for Venture Capital. He was full of passion. He told me about how the travel industry was going to bounce back and how his app was going to revolutionize the way people booked trips.

When I dug into the details, the reality was stark. He had been working on it since February. He had burned through capital. Yet, he had zero sales. He had absolutely nothing to show for it except a belief that the industry will grow.

The Verdict: This is a pipe dream. I wouldn't touch this with a ten-foot pole. If you have no proof of concept—no paying customer—you do not have a business. You have a hobby that loses money. Before you quit your job, you need to prove that someone is willing to open their wallet and pay you for your service.

90% of Startups Fail. Why?

Let's look at the data. 90% of startups fail. 45% of businesses stop operating after five years. Why do they fail? They don't fail because they didn't have a cool logo. They fail because there was no market need, or they ran out of cash trying to find one.

Validation Strategy: Don't Guess, Verify

Before you spend a dollar on a website or a logo, you need to verify that the market actually wants what you are selling. I advise all my clients to perform Market Research before they launch.

You might think your market is huge, but you are likely overestimating it. Here is a practical way to validate your idea using free tools, rather than just guessing.

The Google Trends Test

You need to see if the industry you are entering is dying or growing. Go to Google Trends. Type in the industry you are thinking about entering.

Example A: Roofing Miami - If you look at the trend line for roofing in Florida, it's usually steady. It's flat. That means the demand is consistent. You are competing against everyone else, but the work is there.

Example B: MedSpa - If you type in MedSpa, you might see an explosion in interest. The line is shooting up. That shows you there is a massive opportunity for growth because consumer interest is outpacing the market.

If you see the trend line going down, do not start that business. Past trends indicate you might be in a bit of trouble.

The Competitor Density Check

Next, you need to see who you are fighting. If you want to open a laundromat or a gym, you need to know exactly who is in your radius. I built a tool called the Local Competitor Analysis Tool (which we will discuss in depth later), but the principle is simple: If you are looking to set up a shop, drop a pin on Google Maps in that location. Look at the competitors within a 5-mile radius.

High Threat: If you see competitors with 300+ reviews and 4.8-star ratings, do not open your business there. You will not beat them without a massive budget.

Low Threat: If you see competitors with 3.6-star ratings and reviews complaining about rude staff or broken machines, that is your green light.

You validate your business by finding a gap in the market where the current providers are failing.

The Homeless Test (Calculating Your Risk Tolerance)

Once you have a validated idea, you need to determine if you are the right person to execute it right now. This comes down to Risk Tolerance.

Risk tolerance is exactly what it sounds like: how comfortable are you with the possibility of losing everything? This isn't a complex mathematical formula; it's a simple question I ask potential entrepreneurs: What is the worst-case scenario?

You need to visualize the failure. If everything goes to zero, where do you end up?

Scenario A: The High Risk Tolerance (The 25-Year-Old)

Let's say you are a 25-year-old single male living with your parents. You have $10,000 saved up. You want to start a landscaping business.

The Worst Case: You buy the equipment, you market the business, and nobody calls. You lose your savings. You bruise your ego. You go back to sleeping on the couch and you get a job at a bar.

The Verdict: Go for it. The downside is minimal. You have time to recover.

Scenario B: The Low Risk Tolerance (The Single Mother)

Now, let's say you are a single mother with two kids and a mortgage. You have a steady job paying $60,000 a year. You want to quit to start a consulting firm.

The Worst Case: You quit your job. The clients don't come. You burn through your savings in three months. You miss a mortgage payment. You lose the house. You cannot feed your kids.

The Verdict: Do not quit your job yet. You cannot afford to fail. You must build the side hustle until it replaces your income.

You must be honest with yourself. If the fear of the worst-case scenario paralyzes you, you are not ready to jump. You need to build a bigger safety net first.

The 18-Year-Old Trap (Don't Start Without Skills)

I often get asked by young blokes, I'm 18, I want to start a business. They see the guys on TikTok dropshipping and think that's the path.

The Reality: If you are 18, you likely have no capital and no skills yet. Starting a business without skills is a recipe for disaster. When I was young, I didn't start a tech company. I mowed lawns. I did paper rounds. I worked in a fish and chip shop. I built a skill set first.

My advice to the youth is simple: Get off your ass and learn. Spend your 20s working your tail off. Learn a trade. Learn how to sell. Learn how to manage people on someone else's dime. Once you have a skill—whether that's carpentry, coding, or sales—then you build a business around it.

I'll go on record here: I really hate coaches and individuals who haven't built anything telling people how to build things. It is the most ridiculous thing I have ever heard. Don't be a Founder in your bio if you don't have a product. Be an apprentice. Be a student. Then be a master.

The Financial Reality: Is $10,000 Enough?

A common question I get is, How much money do I need to start?

I conducted a massive study asking 675 successful entrepreneurs what it takes to succeed. I asked them specifically: Is $10,000 enough to start a business? 85% of them said YES.

You do not need a million dollars. You do not need Venture Capital. Most service businesses—cleaning, consulting, landscaping, digital marketing—can be started for significantly less than $10,000. You need a website (maybe $1,500), some legal formation documents, and perhaps some equipment.

However, just because you can start with $10,000 doesn't mean you don't need to know your numbers.

The Break-Even Analysis (Do This Before You Quit)

Whatever you do before you quit your job, make sure you perform a Break-Even Analysis. This is essentially a simple calculation of combining all your expenses to determine exactly how much revenue you need to survive.

Step 1: Tally your personal survival number. Rent, food, utilities. Let's say that is $4,000 a month.

Step 2: Tally your business survival number. Software, insurance, gas, materials. Let's say that is $2,000 a month.

The Number: You need to make $6,000 a month just to exist.

You need to be vigilant with this analysis. I have had clients come to me and say, Ronald, I need $15,000 a month to operate. But when we look through their financial statements, we find out that the rent they thought they were paying has increased. The city fees have increased. They didn't document these changes.

The Interest Rate Trap

If you are buying a building or financing a vehicle, you must factor in interest rate hikes. Generally speaking, every 1% increase in interest rates on a mortgage increases repayments by about 15%. If you calculate your break-even point based on today's rates, and rates go up, you are underwater. Always use the worst-case scenario numbers for your break-even analysis.

The Transition: When to Quit Your Job

So, you have a validated idea, you know your risk tolerance, and you have done the math. When do you actually hand in your resignation letter?

The Side Hustle Strategy

I always recommend starting something on the side of your main gig before taking the leap. If you are working a job and you really don't know when to quit, set something up on the side. Nurture it. Work on it on weekends. See how it progresses.

You quit when two things happen:

Profitability: The side hustle is actually profitable and achieving results. You have real customers paying real money.

The Crossover: The income from the business is consistent enough to cover your Survival Number (from your Break-Even Analysis) for at least 3 months.

The Golden Handcuffs Warning

Be careful of the Golden Handcuffs. I had a question from a guy who was generating $8,000 a month in a side hustle but hated it. He wanted to start another business. He felt trapped because the money was good, but the passion wasn't there. Do not quit your job to build a business you hate. You will work harder in your business than you ever did as an employee. If you don't love the fight, you will quit when it gets hard. And it will get hard.

The Strategy of Focus (Don't Start Two Businesses)

This leads me to a critical rule for new entrepreneurs: Focus on one business endeavor at a time.

If you are young and you have never had a company, do not start multiple companies. I am telling you here and now: please, please listen to me. Do not start multiple companies if you have never built one. It is going to be a shit fight.

Synergy vs. Distraction

Some people think they can start two companies because they are synergistic.

Good Synergy: You start a t-shirt design business, and then you buy the printing shop where the t-shirts are made. That is basically one business with a vertical integration. That works.

Bad Synergy: You start a roofing company and a bookkeeping business. These are completely opposite. They have different challenges, different clients, and different operations. You will fail at both.

If you struggle with managing your time or discipline, starting two businesses is a death sentence for your entrepreneurship career. Focus on one. Build it. Automate it. Then, and only then, do you look at the next one.

Commit to the Grind (The Myth of Balance)

Finally, ignore the BS about work-life balance when you are starting out. If you want to be successful, especially in your early years, you need to work.

When I was building TWECS, my telecommunications company, I worked seven days a week. I missed parties. I missed holidays. I worked 12-hour days minimum. I didn't have a life. I gave up my 20s so I could live the rest of my life how I wanted.

Now, at 33, I can retire if I want to. I don't have a mortgage. I don't have rent. You find balance after you have built the system. You find balance after you have hired the team. If you are looking for balance in year one, you are looking for a job, not a business.

The Work or Work Philosophy

My father always said, As a man, you have two options in life: You can either work, or you can work. That mindset drove me. I did the paper rounds. I bought the family's first TV with a remote control because I hated the turn dial. I learned early that if you do something, you get something out of it.

Success is not given. It is rented, and the rent is due every day. If you aren't willing to pay that rent, stop reading now. But if you are, turn the page. We are going to talk about Money.

KEY TAKEAWAYS

✓ Use the Homeless Test to calculate your true risk tolerance before starting

✓ Validate your idea with Google Trends and competitor density checks

✓ A 'pipe dream' has no market proof—don't bet your savings on hope

✓ Your runway (savings ÷ survival number) determines your strategy

✓ Start as a side hustle until revenue covers 3+ months of expenses

CHAPTER 2: Cash Flow Warfare: Surviving the Service Cycle

There is a saying in business: Revenue is vanity, profit is sanity, but cash is king.

I'm going to take it a step further: If you run out of cash, you are dead. It does not matter how good your website looks. It does not matter if you have five stars on Google. If you cannot make payroll on Friday, you do not have a business; you have a crisis.

Here is a statistic that should keep you awake at night: 20% of profitable businesses fail. Read that again. They are profitable on paper. Their invoices say they made money. But they fail because the cash didn't land in the bank account fast enough to pay the bills. They fail because they ran out of oxygen.

In the service industry—whether you are a roofer, a marketing consultant, or a commercial cleaner—cash flow is often dictated by others. Big companies love to treat small businesses like a bank. They hold your money to boost their own interest earnings while you starve.

This chapter is about waging war on your bank account. We are going to cover the Haram of debt, the mathematical reality of inflation, and the specific protocols you must use to get paid.

The Haram of Debt (and The Interest Rate Trap)

I am a God-fearing man, and I believe usury (charging or paying high interest) is haram. It is a sin because it enslaves the borrower. But even if you aren't religious, debt is a tactical error that tightens the noose around your neck the moment the economy turns against you.

We are living in unprecedented times. Since January 2020, the Federal Reserve has printed over trillions of dollars. When you have that much new money sloshing around in the financial system, you get inflation. And the old definition of inflation isn't just prices going up; it is the artificial increase in the money supply that devalues your hard work.

When inflation rises, central banks raise interest rates to fight it. And when interest rates rise, variable debt becomes a killer.

The $12,000 Mistake (The Math of Debt)

Let's look at a real-world scenario that catches small business owners off guard. Let's say you take out an $85,000 loan for your small business. Maybe it's for a new work truck, a piece of heavy machinery, or a fit-out for a new clinic. You think you can handle the payments at a 5% interest rate over 5 years.

But rates don't stay at 5%. If inflation spikes and you're forced to refinance—or if you have a variable rate loan—and interest rates jump to 10%, your total cost doesn't just go up a little.

On an $85,000 loan over 5 years:

- At 5%, you'll pay roughly $11,200 in total interest over the life of the loan.
- At 10%, you'll pay roughly $23,400 in total interest over the life of the loan.

That is an additional $12,000 gone—money you never budgeted for. That $12,000 was your marketing budget for the year. That was the bonus for your best employee. That was your personal profit. Now, it belongs to the bank. This is why I preach avoiding debt unless absolutely necessary.

Strategy: Owned Assets vs. Financed Fleets

When I had my telecommunications company, TWECS, we were operating up and down the east coast of Australia. We had a fleet of 14 vehicles—trucks, excavators, sucker trucks. Do you know how many were financed? Three.

I owned the rest outright. Why? Because there were nights I lost sleep worrying about finding work for my 30 employees. The construction industry is volatile. Contracts get delayed. Governments change their minds. But I slept a little better knowing that if the contracts dried up tomorrow, nobody could come and tow my trucks away.

If you own your assets, you can park them in the yard during a downturn and they cost you nothing but registration. If you finance them, they eat you alive every single month whether they are working or not.

Alternative Capital: Merchant Financing

If you absolutely must raise capital and you cannot bootstrap it, avoid traditional high-interest loans. Look at Merchant Financing. This is where a lender gives you a lump sum (say, $100,000) and instead of a fixed monthly repayment with compounding interest, they take a percentage of your future invoices—say 20% or 30%—until the amount is paid back.

The Benefit: If you have a slow month and make $0, you pay $0. It aligns the lender's risk with your revenue flow. It is safer than a fixed loan that demands payment even when you are bleeding.

The Enforcer: Getting Paid in Construction & Services

If you are a contractor, you are not a bank. But big companies—especially in construction and corporate services—will treat you like one. They will delay payment for 60, 90, or even 120 days if you let them.

The 90-Day Payment Nightmare

I recall moving my crew from Queensland to Melbourne for a massive project. We were working for a large vendor, a massive company. The payment terms were brutal: 90 days.

Protocol 1: The Kick in the Ass Strategy

You cannot be passive about getting paid. If you have invoices outstanding, you need to follow them up, and you need to follow them up hard. If payment is due on the 30th and it's not there, you do not send a polite email. You call them immediately.

The Script: I'm looking at my accounts. Invoice #104 was due yesterday. I need the payment reference number right now.

The Escalation: If they stall, you ask for the accounts payable manager. You do not get off the phone until you have a date and a reference number. Don't let bad debts accumulate. Recover them fast or send them to collections.

Protocol 2: Stop Work Authority

I have sat in meetings with executives of ASX-listed companies (the Australian equivalent of the New York Stock Exchange) and looked them in the eye. I told them: You owe me this money. Pay me, or we stop working. Or I take you to court.

It is uncomfortable. It is aggressive. But you must be willing to stop the tools. If you continue working for a client who hasn't paid you, you are digging your own grave. You are increasing your exposure to a bad debtor. Stop the work. It usually magically speeds up the payment process.

Protocol 3: Pre-Payments and Call-Out Fees

If you are a service business like a plumber, an electrician, or an IT consultant, stop working for free. Move to pre-payments where possible.

The Rule: Charge a call-out fee before you even start the truck.

The Logic: If you charge a $150 call-out fee upfront, you cover your fuel and time. If the client ghosts you later on the remaining $300 balance, it hurts, but it doesn't kill you. You aren't chasing the full $450. You have mitigated your risk.

Protocol 4: The Escrow Protection (For Large Projects)

If you are taking on a massive contract that could sink your business if the client defaults, use an Escrow Service or a Trust.

How it works: The client pays the money into a third-party account (the intermediary). The money is there. You can see it. But you can't touch it, and neither can they.

The Safety: You do the work knowing the money exists. Once the work is verified, the trustee releases the funds. This prevents the I don't have the cash right now excuse after you have already installed the expensive equipment.

The Cash Flow Forecast: Seeing the Future

If you can't answer the question: Will I have cash in 3 months? you are driving blindfolded at 100 miles per hour. You need a system. I have built a Free Cash Flow Template that you must use to survive.

Most business owners look at their bank balance today and think they are rich. They forget that the quarterly tax bill is due in six weeks, the insurance renewal is due in two months, and three staff members are going on holiday.

How to Execute a 12-Month Forecast

Step 1: The Transaction Log

You need to record every single inflow and outflow. Do not just lump things together.

- Inflows: Customer payments, retention releases (if you are in construction), merchant financing injections.
- Outflows: Payroll, materials, equipment hire, rent, software subscriptions.
- The Discipline: Put a minus sign before expenses (e.g., -35,000). This allows the spreadsheet to calculate your burn rate automatically.

Step 2: The Negative Equity Warning System

The beauty of a 12-month view is that it spots the iceberg before you hit it. You might look at the dashboard and see that in October, your cumulative cash line dips below $0.

The Action: Because you are seeing this in July, you have three months to fix it. You can delay a truck purchase. You can run a Cash Injection marketing offer to get pre-payments. You can fire a non-performing employee.

The Result: You avoid bankruptcy because you saw the dip coming. If you wait until October to look at the bank account, it is too late.

Step 3: The Tax Calculator

My template includes a built-in tax calculator. A massive mistake small businesses make is spending their tax money. They see $10,000 in the bank and think it is theirs. No. $3,000 of that belongs to the government. If you do not segregate that money mentally and physically in your forecast, you will get to tax time and have to take out a high-interest loan just to pay the IRS. That is the death spiral.

Pricing Your Services: The Inflation Shield

Finally, you cannot win the cash flow war if you are underpricing your services. 85% of small business owners are concerned about inflation. The only way to beat inflation is to price above it.

If you have been in business for two years and haven't raised your prices, you are effectively paying your customers to work for them. Your gas has gone up. Your insurance has gone up (premiums rose by 20% recently). Your software costs have gone up.

The ROI Pricing Model

Stop pricing based on hours. Price based on Value and ROI.

The Wrong Pitch: I charge $100 an hour. (The client thinks: Can you do it in 30 minutes?)

The Right Pitch: I will generate you $5,000 in new revenue. My fee is $1,000.

When you frame it this way, the client doesn't care if it takes you 1 hour or 10 hours. They care about the $4,000 profit. This allows you to increase your margins significantly without the client feeling ripped off.

The Annual Increase Protocol

You need to train your clients to expect price rises. Increase your prices by 5% to 10% annually. Most clients will not push back on 5%. It matches their expectation of inflation.

The Warning: Do not get greedy. I knew a business owner who tried to double their prices overnight (100% increase) because they wanted to work less and make more. They lost almost every single client and had to beg for work. Be consistent, be fair, but do not be cheap.

Competitor Pricing Check

Before you set your prices, call five competitors. Ask for a quote on a standard job. If the average market rate is $2,500 and you are charging $1,500, you are not being competitive. You are leaving $1,000 on the table for every single job. You are signaling that your quality is lower. Raise your price to the market average immediately.

Summary: The Rules of Cash Flow Warfare

Debt is a weapon that often points back at you. Avoid it. If you must use it, ensure it is fixed-rate or flexible like merchant financing.

Enforce your payment terms. Be the squeaky wheel. Stop work if they don't pay. Get paid upfront for service calls.

Forecast or fail. Use the 12-month tracker. If you can't see 90 days ahead, you are flying blind.

Price for profit. Raise your prices by 5-10% every year. Do not apologize for it. It is the cost of survival.

You are in business to make a profit, not to handle money for other people. Protect your cash flow as if your life depends on it—because your business's life certainly does.

KEY TAKEAWAYS

✓ Cash flow kills more businesses than lack of profit

✓ Use a 12-month rolling cash flow forecast—update it weekly

✓ Avoid debt where possible; if needed, use merchant financing over bank loans

✓ Enforce payment terms ruthlessly—be the squeaky wheel

✓ The 50/30/20 rule: 50% operations, 30% growth, 20% reserves

CHAPTER 3: The Lead Engine: Data Over Hope & The Science of the Hunt

Most service business owners treat lead generation like gambling. They throw money at Facebook Ads, they buy a billboard, or they pay for shared leads from a third-party site, and then they sit by the phone hoping it rings.

Hope is not a strategy. Data is a strategy.

If you are running a business based on hope, you are already dead; you just haven't closed the doors yet. In the military, we didn't fire our weapons blindly into the dark hoping to hit an enemy. We used reconnaissance. We identified targets. We calculated windage and elevation. We fired with precision.

Your marketing must be the same.

I conducted a massive study asking 675 successful entrepreneurs a simple question: Should a business invest in marketing? A staggering 94.3% said YES. But here is the problem: while almost everyone agrees they should be marketing, most have no idea where their money is actually going. They are guessing.

In this chapter, we are going to build your Lead Engine. We are going to move away from posting and praying to a system based on hard financial data. We are going to cover the mathematical reality of SEO vs. Paid Ads, how to use spy tools to dismantle your local competitors, and how to use Guerrilla Warfare tactics on Reddit to find customers for free.

The Financial Reality: SEO vs. Paid Ads (The ROI Math)

Before you spend a single dollar, you need to understand the Return on Investment (ROI). I have an MBA in finance, so I don't look at likes or impressions. I look at the bank account.

I track data across hundreds of clients in industries ranging from roofing to chiropractic care. Here is the hard reality of the numbers you are up against.

The PPC Trap (Pay-Per-Click)

If you are running Google Ads or Facebook Ads, you are renting attention. The moment you stop paying, the leads stop coming.

The Statistic: For every $1 you spend on Pay-Per-Click (PPC) ads, the average successful campaign generates about $1.20 in return.

The Reality: That is a 20% margin. That is razor-thin. If you mess up your targeting, or if your sales team misses a few calls, you are instantly losing money. If you have a budget under $1,500 a month, stay away from paid ads. You will get eaten alive by the big players who can afford to bleed cash to acquire a customer.

The SEO Wealth Builder (Search Engine Optimization)

SEO is the asset you own. It is the real estate of the internet.

The Statistic: For every $1 you spend on legitimate, high-quality SEO, you typically see a return of $5 to $8.

The Reality: That is a 500% to 800% return. Why is it so much higher? Because of Intent.

Intent vs. Interruption

When you run a Facebook Ad, you are engaging in Interruption Marketing. You are popping up while someone is trying to look at photos of their grandkids or watch a cat video. They don't want a plumber right now. You are annoying them.

When you rank #1 on Google, you are capitalizing on Intent. When someone types Emergency Roofer Fort Lauderdale into Google, they have a problem, they are stressed, and they have a credit card in their hand. They are looking for you.

The Verdict: Paid ads are for speed. SEO is for wealth. If you are a service business, your primary objective must be to own the organic search results.

Tactical Tool: The Local Competitor Analysis (Reconnaissance)

You cannot win a war if you don't know who you are fighting. Most business owners think they know their competitors. They say, Oh yeah, Bob's Plumbing down the street. I'll bet you $100 you don't actually know who is winning on Google in your specific neighborhood.

I built a specific Local Competitor Analysis Tool that connects to the Google Places API. It scrapes data to tell you exactly who is stealing your customers and, more importantly, where they are weak.

How to Execute a Competitive Analysis

Step 1: The Pin Drop Strategy

Do not just search your city name (e.g., Miami). That is too broad. You need to be precise. Go to Google Maps. Right-click on the exact street corner or neighborhood you want to dominate—let's say it's near the Sports Complex in Jupiter, Florida. Copy the Latitude and Longitude coordinates. Paste those coordinates into the Input tab of the free tool. Set your search radius to 3 to 5 miles.

Step 2: The Threat Level Assessment

Click Run Competitor Analysis. In about 20 seconds, the tool will pull up to 200 competitors in that radius and assign them a Threat Level based on their reviews and ratings.

- High Threat: These are the competitors with 300+ reviews and a 4.8-star rating. They are entrenched. They have a war chest. Do not try to fight them head-on unless you have a massive budget.
- Low Threat: These are the competitors with 3.6 stars and 184 reviews. This is where you strike.

Step 3: The Review Gap Opportunity

I once looked at a laundromat location near Pembroke Pines using this exact method. The closest competitor was a Low Threat. I looked at their reviews. Customers were screaming in the comments: Worst place I've ever been, Ripped off $5 to wash, Machines out of service.

This is a goldmine. If you see a competitor with bad reviews near a residential area, you have found a gap in the line. You enter that market. You offer clean machines. You offer a smile. You reply to reviews. You will crush them because they have already alienated the customer base.

Use the tool to find the weak spots on the map, and set up your perimeter there.

Tactical Tool: The Reddit Scraper (Guerilla Warfare)

Most of your competitors are lazy. They are fighting over the same leads on HomeAdvisor or Thumbtack, paying $50 for a lead that gets sold to five other people. We are not going to do that. We are going to go where people are asking for help unfiltered. We are going to use Reddit.

People go to Facebook to brag. They go to Instagram to look pretty. They go to Reddit to solve problems. If you are an accountant, there are people on Reddit right now asking, How do I pay my small business taxes? If you are a roofer, homeowners are posting photos of leaks asking, Is this quote for $15,000 fair?

I built a Free Reddit Scraper Tool to mine this gold. Here is the exact Standard Operating Procedure (SOP) on how to use it to fill your pipeline without spending a dime on ads.

Phase 1: The Setup

Download the Reddit Scraper Sheet.

Go to the Setup tab. You need a free Reddit API key. Don't panic; it takes 2 minutes. Click the link provided in the sheet, select Script, and copy the Client ID and Client Secret.

Paste them into the sheet. You now have a custom software tool that would cost you $200/month elsewhere, running for free.

Phase 2: The Keyword Hunt

Do not just search for your industry name. Search for the Pain.

- Wrong Search: Accountant.

- Right Search: Pay Tax, IRS Help, Tax Audit, Payroll Issues.
- Right Search (Contractors): Roof Leak, Quote help, Plumbing cost.

Enter these keywords into the Config tab. Set the search to Top Level to find the original posts.

Phase 3: The Engagement Filter

Click Run Scrape. The tool will pull hundreds of threads. Now, look at the Engagement Score.

- High Engagement: These are viral posts. This is market research. Read the comments to see what people hate about your industry. If everyone is complaining that Roofers never call back, you make your slogan The Roofer That Calls Back.
- Low Engagement (The Sniper Targets): Look for posts with zero comments. This person is screaming into the void. They have a problem, and nobody has helped them.

Phase 4: The Sniper Outreach

The tool gives you the direct URL to the user's profile.

- Do Not: Spam them with Hire me. You will get banned.
- Do: Send a Direct Message (DM).

Script: Hey, I saw your post about struggling with payroll tax. It can be a nightmare. Here is exactly how you fix it: [Insert 2-sentence solution]. If you need help filing next quarter so you don't get fined, let me know.

This approach builds trust immediately because you led with value. It costs you $0.

Strategy: The 250+ Directory Safety Net

Most small businesses list themselves on Google and Facebook and stop there. That is lazy, and it is costing you money. According to my estimates, you could be missing out on 5 to 10 additional leads every single month simply because you aren't listed on niche specific directories.

Why Directories Matter

Traffic: Some people still use YellowPages, MapQuest, or the Better Business Bureau (BBB). If you aren't there, you don't exist to them.

SEO (The Real Reason): Google trusts businesses that are listed everywhere. These are called Citations. If your business name, address, and phone number (NAP) appear consistently on 200+ websites, Google treats you as a legitimate authority. This pushes your website higher in the rankings.

The Execution: I have compiled a Master List of 250+ Business Directories.

- General: Yelp, Bing Places, Yahoo Local, Nextdoor.
- Industry Specific: Roofers: GAF, Porch, Houzz. Medical: HealthGrades, RateMDs.
- Data Aggregators: Get listed on Data Aggregators like WhiteSpark or BrightLocal. These services push your information out to hundreds of smaller directories automatically.

Action Step: Download the directory list. Spend one hour a week knocking out 10 listings. In 6 months, you will be everywhere.

Strategy: B2B Whale Hunting (The Lead Generator Tool)

If you are a B2B business (Recruiter, Commercial Cleaner, Marketing Agency) or a Contractor looking for commercial work, you cannot wait for the phone to ring. You need to hunt. I call this Whale Hunting. Instead of catching one small fish (a homeowner), you catch a whale (a partner who sends you 50 jobs).

The Logic: If you are a landscaper, stop chasing homeowners. Chase Real Estate Agents. One Real Estate Agent manages 20+ listings a year. Every listing needs a cleanup before photos. One relationship = 20 jobs.

The Tool: I built a Client Lead Generator that scrapes Google Maps to find these partners for you.

How to Execute the Whale Hunting Strategy

1. Configure the Generator: Open the Client Lead Generator sheet. Select Real Estate Agencies from the dropdown menu (it holds over 260 industries). Select your location (e.g., Fort Lauderdale, FL).

2. The Filter (The Goldilocks Zone): Click Find Leads. In about 30 seconds, it will scrape Google Maps and give you a list of 150+ agencies. Now, filter the results by Review Count.

- Avoid the Giants: The agency with 1,000 reviews has gatekeepers. You will never get the owner on the phone.

- Avoid the Ghosts: The agency with 2 reviews is probably dead.

- Target the Middle: Look for agencies with 20 to 50 reviews. These are active, hungry businesses. They are big enough to pay you, but small enough that the owner still answers the phone.

3. The Hot Lunch Pitch: Do not email them asking for work. Call them.

Script: Hey, I see you're doing a lot of volume in Fort Lauderdale. I'm a local landscaper. I specialize in pre-listing cleanups. I noticed you have a 4.8-star rating, so I know you care about quality. I want to be your go-to guy when you need a property ready for an open house. Can I buy you lunch and show you my portfolio?

A $50 lunch will generate more revenue than $5,000 in Google Ads because trust is built face-to-face. This tool costs about $0.50 to run using the API. It is cheaper than a gumball.

Summary: Your Marching Orders

We have covered the mechanics of the Lead Engine.

Stop Gambling: If you have less than $1,500/month, kill your paid ads. Focus on SEO and organic outreach.

Reconnaissance: Use the Local Competitor Tool. Find the weak competitor with 3.6 stars and set up shop next door to steal their unhappy customers.

Sniper Fire: Use the Reddit Scraper. Find the people asking How much does a roof cost? and answer them directly.

Safety Net: Get listed on the 250+ Directories to boost your SEO authority.

Whale Hunting: Use the Lead Generator. Find the Real Estate Agents or Property Managers who can feed you work for years.

Lead generation is not a mystery. It is a process. It is a machine. Now that you have the blueprints, go build the engine.

KEY TAKEAWAYS

✓ Your database is your most valuable asset—build it obsessively

✓ Use the Local Competitor Analysis Tool to find gaps in your market

✓ SEO and Google Business Profile are long-term investments that compound

✓ Track every lead source so you know where to double down

✓ Speed to lead matters—respond within 5 minutes or lose the job

CHAPTER 4: The Kill: Sales, Pricing & The Art of the Proposal

You have executed the reconnaissance. You have used the Reddit Scraper to find the bleeding necks. You have used the Competitor Analysis tool to find the weak spots in the enemy lines. You have the leads.

Now comes the hard part.

You can generate all the leads in the world, but if you can't close them, you are just practicing for bankruptcy. Sales is where the rubber meets the road. It is where your bank account actually changes.

Most service business owners are terrified of sales. They think sales is about tricking people. They send out a quote, the client ghosts them, and they give up. They say, Oh well, the lead wasn't serious.

Wrong. The lead was serious. You just failed to engage.

In this chapter, we are going to cover The Kill. We are going to discuss the mathematical necessity of the follow-up, how to price your services so you actually make a profit, and the psychological warfare involved in getting a signed contract and a 5-star review.

The Follow-Up Protocol: The Math of Survival

Let's start with a statistic that should make you sick to your stomach if you are currently sending one email and giving up.

80% of sales happen after the 5th to 7th contact.

Yet, almost every business owner I coach stops after the first or second attempt. They send the quote. They wait two days. They send one polite email: Just checking in. Then they go silent because they don't want to be annoying.

If you stop at touchpoint #2, you are leaving 80% of your revenue on the table for your competitor who is willing to be annoying.

The Mathematics of Persistence (Lowering Your CPA)

You might be thinking, Ronald, I don't have time to chase people. You don't understand the math. Following up doesn't just get you more sales; it drastically lowers your Cost Per Acquisition (CPA).

Let me break this down with a mathematical formula so you can see exactly how much money you are burning by being lazy.

The Scenario: Let's say you are running a Google Ads campaign. You spend $1,000 to generate 10 leads. Your Cost Per Lead (CPL) is $100.

The Lazy Operator (1-2 Follow-ups): You call the 10 leads once. You convert 1 of them.

- Total Spend: $1,000
- Total Customers: 1
- Cost Per Acquisition (CPA): $1,000
- Result: You paid $1,000 to get one client. If that client only pays you $800, you have lost money. You are bleeding out.

The War Manual Operator (5-7 Follow-ups): You take those same 10 leads. You didn't spend a penny more on ads. But you implement a Set and Forget follow-up system (SMS and Email) that touches them 7 times over 2 weeks. Because you stayed top-of-mind, you convert 3 of them instead of 1.

- Total Spend: $1,000
- Total Customers: 3
- Cost Per Acquisition (CPA): $333

The Outcome: By simply increasing your follow-up, you have dropped your cost to acquire a customer from $1,000 down to $333.

You are now three times more profitable than your competitor, using the exact same leads. This is how you win. You don't need cheaper leads; you need a better bucket that doesn't leak.

How to Build the Set and Forget System

You cannot do this manually. You will forget. You need a system. I have built a Lead Nurturing Email Blueprint that you can use, but here is the logic of how to set it up using basic tools (even a simple CRM or Gmail templates).

The 7-Point Touch Sequence:

Day 0 (Immediate): The Auto-Responder. Thanks for the inquiry. I'm reviewing your details.

Day 1 (Call + SMS): You call. If they don't answer, you send an SMS immediately: Hey [Name], it's Ronald. Just tried to call you about the roof estimate. When is a good time to chat?

Day 2 (Email - Value): Don't just say buy my stuff. Send them a case study. Hey, we just finished a job down the street from you. Check out the before and after.

Day 3 (SMS): Hey [Name], just checking you got the quote? I have a slot open next Tuesday for an inspection.

Day 5 (Email - The No Question): Are you still interested in fixing your [Problem], or should I close this file? (People hate having files closed on them; they will reply).

Day 7 (Call): Final manual attempt.

Day 14 (The Breakup Email): I haven't heard back, so I assume you've gone in a different direction. I'll take you off my list.

If you implement this sequence, you will triple your sales. It is not magic; it is volume.

The Hidden Markup Strategy: Pricing for Profit

Now that you have the client on the hook, you need to send them a quote. Here is a mistake I see contractors make every single day: They show their markup.

If you send a quote that breaks down:

- Materials Cost: $1,000
- My Markup (20%): $200
- Labor: $1,000

The client immediately looks at that $200 and thinks, Why am I paying you $200 just to go to Home Depot? I can buy the materials myself. You have just invited them to negotiate against your profit margin.

The Fix: You must hide your markup inside the unit cost. I have built a Free Contractor Quote Template (available in the toolkit) that does this automatically. Here is the technical deep dive on how to use it to protect your margins.

Step-by-Step SOP: The Hidden Markup

1. The Setup (Settings Tab): Open the spreadsheet. Go to the Settings tab. Enter your company details and your local sales tax rate (e.g., 7% in Florida).

2. The Database (Materials Tab): Go to the Materials tab. This is your database. You are going to build your line items here.

- Item Code: Create a code, e.g., MAT-005.
- Description: 3-inch Gal Nails (Box).
- Unit Cost: Enter exactly what you pay at the supplier. Let's say $75.
- The Secret Weapon (Markup Column): In the column labeled Markup, enter your desired margin. I recommend 0.20 (20%).

3. The Calculation: The spreadsheet will automatically calculate the Client Price. $75 (Cost) + $15 (20% markup) = $90 (Client Price). You see the $90. You see the $75. You know you are making $15 profit on that box of nails.

4. Building the Quote: Go to the Quote Builder tab. Select MAT-005 from the dropdown. The sheet pulls in the price of $90. It asks you for the quantity. You type 2. Total: $180.

5. The Client Proposal (The Magic Trick): Click on the Client Proposal tab. This is the version you print or PDF to send to the client.

Crucial Point: On this document, the Markup column does not exist. The client sees: 3-inch Gal Nails - Unit Price: $90. They do not see that you paid $75. They accept $90 as the market rate. They cannot argue with you about your profit because they cannot see it.

6. The Profitability Check (The Actuals): Once the job is done, you must use the Job Profitability tab. You quoted $13,612. You enter your actual receipts. Did you spend $8,500? The sheet calculates the variance. If you have a positive variance, you made extra profit. If you have a negative variance, you know next time you need to raise your markup to 25%.

This tool stops clients from nickel-and-diming you and ensures you actually make the 20-30% profit margin you need to survive.

The Hot Lunch Strategy: The $50 B2B Tactic

If you are a B2B business (commercial cleaner, marketing agency, commercial contractor), or if you are looking for referral partners (like Real Estate Agents for landscapers), stop spending $5,000 on Google Ads.

You are wasting money trying to digitally target one person. Instead, use the Hot Lunch Strategy.

The Logic: A Real Estate Agent manages 20+ properties. A Strata Manager manages 50+ buildings. One relationship with them is worth 50 individual leads. You don't need 1,000 views on a Facebook ad; you need one lunch with one decision-maker.

The Protocol:

Identify the Target: Use the Client Lead Generator (from Chapter 3) to find Real Estate Agencies in your zip code. Look for the ones with 20-50 reviews (they are active but not too big to ignore you).

The Approach: Call them. Do not email.

The Script: Hey [Name], I'm a local landscaper/cleaner. I see you guys are moving a lot of property in [Area]. I want to be your go-to guy for pre-sale prep. I know you're busy, so I want to buy you lunch—my treat—just to introduce myself and show you my portfolio. No hard sell, I just want to feed you and see if I can help you out.

The Cost: This will cost you $50 to $70 for a decent lunch.

The Return: People rarely say no to a free lunch. When you sit down face-to-face, you build trust that no website can match. If that agent sends you 10 jobs a year at $500 each, that $50 lunch just generated $5,000 in revenue.

Compare that to Google Ads, where you might spend $5,000 to get the same result. The Hot Lunch is the highest ROI marketing strategy for local service businesses. Period.

The Jimmy Script: Psychology of the 5-Star Review

You have closed the deal. You have done the work. You have been paid. The job isn't over. You need the Review.

93% of consumers read online reviews before making a purchase. If you have 5 reviews and your competitor has 58, you lose. Even if your work is better.

Most business owners ask for reviews the wrong way. They send an automated email 3 days later saying, Please leave us a review. The client ignores it. You need to ask in person, at the peak of happiness, using a specific psychological trigger: Altruism.

People don't care about your business. They care about their community. You need to make the review about helping their neighbors, not helping you.

The Jimmy Script: When you are doing the final walkthrough (or final handover), and the client is smiling, you say this:

Jimmy, thank you for choosing me as your roofing contractor. I know there are a lot of others out there vying for your business, and I'm grateful you went with my company. We want to ensure that your neighbors, friends, and family work with roofers whom you know they can trust. Leaving us a review can help them in the future.

Why this works:

Gratitude: You thank them first.

Validation: You acknowledge they had choices.

The Hero Arc: You shift the focus. You aren't asking for a favor for you; you are asking them to protect their neighbors from bad contractors. You make Jimmy the hero of his cul-de-sac.

Removing the Friction (The QR Code)

Jimmy says, Sure, I'll do it later. (He won't). You say: I've made it super easy. I've got a QR code right here.

The Setup:

Go to your Google Business Profile. Click Get More Reviews. Copy the link.

Paste that link into a QR Code Generator (I have a free tool for this linked in the toolkit).

Save the QR code image to your phone as a Favorite photo, or print it on a card.

Show Jimmy the code. Just scan this with your camera. It takes 5 seconds.

It opens the review box directly. He taps 5 stars. He writes, Ronald was great. Done. You just banked an asset that will pay you dividends for years.

Summary: The Kill Box

You now have a complete closing system.

The Follow-Up: You are going to touch every lead 5 to 7 times using SMS and Email, dropping your CPA from $1,000 to $333. You will stop being lazy.

The Pricing: You are going to use the Contractor Quote Template to hide your 20% markup inside the unit cost, so clients stop stealing your profit.

The Hot Lunch: You are going to spend $50 to buy a Real Estate Agent lunch, securing a referral partner for life.

The Jimmy Script: You are going to get the review on-site, every time, by making the client a hero to their neighbors.

Execute this, and you won't just be busy. You will be profitable.

KEY TAKEAWAYS

✓ Price based on value delivered, not hours worked

✓ The 3-option proposal: Bronze, Silver, Gold—most pick the middle

✓ Follow up relentlessly: 80% of sales happen after the 5th contact

✓ Objection handling is about listening, not convincing

✓ Your proposal is a sales document, not just a quote

CHAPTER 5: The Platoon: Hiring, Firing & The $130,000 Mistake

There is a saying in the military: The standard you walk past is the standard you accept.

If you see a soldier with their boots unpolished or their rifle dirty, and you say nothing, you have just set a new, lower standard for the entire platoon. You have told them that mediocrity is acceptable.

In business, this is doubly true. You can be the best salesman in the world, and you can have the best lead generation systems (which we covered in Chapter 3), but if you hire the wrong people to execute the work, your reputation will be destroyed faster than you can rebuild it.

Your team will make or break you. They will either be the reason you can finally take a holiday and sleep soundly, or they will be the reason you wake up at 3:00 AM in a cold sweat, wondering if the job site is on fire.

I have hired over 250 people in my career. I have hired family. I have hired friends. I have hired strangers. And I have lost $130,000 making the wrong choice because I ignored the process.

This chapter is about building your platoon. It is about the math of hiring, the reality of firing, and the controversial truth about working with family.

The $130,000 Lesson (Don't Hire a Friend Without a Process)

I want to tell you about the most expensive lesson I ever learned. It wasn't a bad stock trade, and it wasn't a lawsuit. It was a hire.

When my telecommunications company, TWECS, was expanding, we decided to move aggressively into the civil construction space. We were doing well, digging trenches and laying fiber, but I wanted to scale. I needed someone to run that specific division because I couldn't be everywhere at once.

I had a mate—a good guy—who had experience in this exact area. He had run his own business before; he had his own employees in the past. On paper, and in my mind, he was the perfect fit.

I thought, Perfect. I know him. I trust him. I don't need to do the formal interview process. We can skip the vetting. We can skip the reference checks because I know him.

That was the lie.

I hired him based on friendship, not on a rigorous assessment of his current capability. At the time, he was going through some personal troubles at home. Now, because of my background in the Australian Army, I have seen a lot of mates go through hard times. In the military, you pull your mates through. You carry their pack. I believed that if I gave him this opportunity, he would overcome his personal issues and crush it for me.

I was wrong.

Because I didn't vet him professionally, I didn't realize that his head wasn't in the game. He couldn't handle the pressure. He made mistakes on site. He missed critical deadlines. And because he was a friend, I let it slide longer than I would have for a stranger. If a stranger messed up that badly in week one, I would have fired them. But because it was a mate, I made excuses. He's going through a tough time, I told myself. He'll turn it around.

He didn't turn it around.

By the time I finally pulled the plug, the damage was catastrophic. We are talking about $130,000 in cold hard cash lost due to errors, rework, and lost productivity. If you factor in the opportunity cost—the jobs we missed because we were fixing his mess—the loss was probably closer to a quarter of a million dollars.

But the money wasn't the worst part. The worst part was the screaming match on the phone. The worst part was the breakdown of the relationship.

The Lesson: Never hire someone just because you like them. The business doesn't care about your feelings. You must have a vetting process, even for friends. If you cannot look a friend in the eye and say, You are not hitting your KPIs, and if you don't fix it by Friday, you are fired, then you cannot hire that friend.

The Case for Hiring Family (The $50 Night Out)

Now, let's flip the coin. You will hear gurus and MBA professors tell you, Never hire family. It's a recipe for disaster.

I disagree. In fact, I will go on record saying I would not be where I am today without my family.

My younger brother and a mate from the Army were my first two employees. When my company was at its peak, I had four family members working for me, including my brother and cousins.

Here is the difference between hiring a friend blindly and hiring family the right way: Loyalty.

When the chips are down, a mercenary (a stranger hired for a paycheck) will leave you for an extra $2 an hour. Family—if you have a good family—will bleed for you.

The Story of the $50 Note

Let me paint you a picture of what real loyalty looks like. My brother and I had just moved from Queensland down to Melbourne for a massive project. We were working for a large vendor, a massive company listed on the stock exchange. You would think they would pay on time. You would be wrong. The payment terms were brutal: 90 days.

We had moved our lives down there. We were working 12-hour days, 7 days a week. We were exhausting ourselves to get this project off the ground. But because of the payment terms, we were technically broke. We had maybe $200 left in the company account to get us through the week for food and fuel.

I remember one specific evening vividly. My younger brother came up to me. He was young, in his early 20s. His mates were going out clubbing, and he wanted to go with them. He had worked a 60-hour week. He deserved his paycheck.

But he knew the situation. He didn't demand his full wage. He didn't quit because the money was tight. He didn't threaten to go to the labor board. He asked me for $50.

He took that $50, went out, had his night, and was back at work the next day grinding. That is loyalty. That is blood. A stranger would have walked off the job. My brother stayed.

When the big check finally landed—a $91,000 payment—I made sure he got a massive bonus. I looked after him for his entire career with me because he looked after me when I had nothing.

The Rules of Engagement for Family

Hiring family works, but only if you set Boundaries. If you hire family without rules, you end up with a Lazy Cousin situation where they sit on their phone, distract the team, and ruin your authority.

The Hat Conversation: You must sit them down before day one and say: From 7:00 AM to 5:00 PM, I am not your brother; I am your boss. If you slack off, you are disrespecting the business and the food on my table. After 5:00 PM, I am your brother again.

No Handouts: They must be the right fit for the job. Do not invent a job for your cousin just because he needs cash. If they aren't qualified, they don't get the seat.

Lead from the Front: You cannot expect family to respect you if you are lazy. If you are the first one in the warehouse and the last one to leave, they will follow you. If you sit in the air conditioning while they dig holes, they will resent you.

The Employee Cost Calculator: The Math of Survival

Whether you hire family or strangers, you need to understand the math. One of the biggest fears I hear from service business owners is: Can I actually afford to hire someone?

Most owners calculate this using Napkin Math. They think: Okay, I pay him $25 an hour. He works 40 hours. That's $1,000 a week. I can afford $1,000.

This is wrong. And if you bid on a project using this math, you will lose money.

I have built a specific tool called the Employee Cost Calculator. You need to use this because the Real Cost of an employee is often 1.5x to 2x their hourly wage.

How to Use the Employee Cost Calculator

1. The Fully Loaded Cost: Open the calculator. Input the base salary. Now, look at the additional fields. You must account for Payroll Taxes and Benefits. In the US, this can add 15-20% immediately. Then, input the Equipment Costs. Does this new hire need a van? A laptop? A set of tools? A uniform? That $5,000 upfront cost needs to be amortized into your decision.

2. The Hidden Killer: Training Time: This is where everyone fails. When you hire a new guy, you lose productivity. If you are billing $150 an hour, and you spend 20 hours in the first month training the new guy, you have just lost $3,000 of your own revenue. You must input your own hourly rate into the calculator to see the Opportunity Cost of training.

3. The Cash Flow Dip (The Death Valley): The calculator has a Monthly Projections tab. It shows you exactly what happens to your bank balance in Month 1, Month 2, and Month 3. Almost always, Month 1 is a loss. You are paying salary, buying equipment, and paying for training, but the employee isn't generating revenue yet. The calculator will give you a warning: Caution: ROI is negative in this timeframe. You need to know this. If you have $10,000 in the bank and the Dip costs $12,000, hiring this person will bankrupt you before they ever become profitable.

4. Revenue Modeling: The tool allows you to toggle between Hourly Billing, Jobs Per Month, or Revenue Per Employee.

- For Contractors: Use Jobs Per Month. If you hire a new crew lead, how many extra roof installs can you do? If the answer is zero, why are you hiring him?
- For Professional Services: Use Billable Hours. If a paralegal frees up 10 hours of your time, can you bill those 10 hours at your attorney rate?

Why This Matters for Project Tenders: If you are a contractor putting in a tender for a commercial job, and you use the Napkin Math ($25/hour), you will win the bid, do the work, and realize at the end that you made zero profit because you forgot to factor in the workers' comp, the training time, and the equipment wear and tear. Use the calculator. Know your numbers to the penny.

The Weekend Team Hack: Staffing the Graveyard Shift

If you run a retail store, a restaurant, or a service business that operates 7 days a week, you know the struggle: Nobody wants to work weekends.

You hire a Weekend Team, but they are unreliable. They call in sick on Sunday morning because they are hungover. They quit after two weeks. You are constantly scrambling to cover shifts.

The problem isn't the people; it's the Incentive Structure. You are asking people to give up their social life for the same money they could make on a Tuesday. Why would they do that?

The Split Budget Hack

I learned this when managing crews that had to work unsociable hours. You solve this with money, but you do it without increasing your total budget.

The Scenario: Let's say you need coverage 7 days a week.

- Current State: You have 10 employees. You pay them all $20 an hour.
- Total Hourly Budget: $200 per operating hour (spread across the team).

The Hack: On Saturday and Sunday, you do not need 10 people standing around. The traffic might be slightly different, or the tasks are different.

- New Strategy: Cut the weekend team size to 5 people.
- The Compensation: Take that same $200 budget and divide it by the 5 people.
- New Wage: $40 an hour.

The Result: Suddenly, your employees are fighting to work weekends. You have turned the graveyard shift into the goldmine shift. You are now paying double the market rate. You will attract the best talent. They will show up on time because they don't want to lose the $40/hour gig.

Note: Even if you can't double it, even a 50% increase makes a massive difference.

The Buy-In Factor: This solves the issue of Buy-In. When I had my construction company, I had to get guys to work in the mud, in the rain, on weekends. You cannot force buy-in with a speech about company culture. You buy buy-in with cash and respect. By paying them significantly more for the harder shifts, you are showing them respect. You are acknowledging that their Sunday is valuable. In return, they give you reliability.

Firing: The Passive-Aggressive Trap

Finally, once you have your platoon, you must maintain standards. I see a lot of weak managers who are afraid to fire people. Instead of having the hard conversation, they do something toxic: The Triple Workload Trap.

They want the employee to quit, so they triple their workload without increasing their pay. They try to make the employee's life miserable so the employee resigns. Do not do this. It is cowardly, and it poisons your company culture. The other employees see this. They see that you are not a leader who is direct; you are a manipulator.

The Correct Way to Fire:

Document the Failure: You were hired to do X. You are doing Y. Here is the data.

The Opportunity: Can you fix this? If not, we have a problem.

The Cut: If they are not capable, or if they have a bad attitude, fire them. Do it quickly. Do it respectfully. But do it.

Summary

- Hiring friends without a process is a $130,000 gambling habit. Don't do it.
- Hiring family is a superpower, provided you have clear boundaries and you reward loyalty.
- Use the Employee Cost Calculator. If the math doesn't work on the spreadsheet, it won't work in reality.
- Fix your weekend staffing issues by concentrating your budget on fewer, better-paid people.

Your team is your engine. If you put sand in the engine (bad hires), the car stops. If you put high-octane fuel in (great hires, incentives, and loyalty), you win the race.

KEY TAKEAWAYS
✓ Hire slow, fire fast—the $130,000 mistake proves it

✓ Never hire friends or family unless you can fire them

✓ Use a scorecard for every hire—remove emotion from the decision

✓ Culture fit matters as much as skills—one bad apple poisons the team

✓ Document everything: job descriptions, KPIs, and performance reviews

CHAPTER 6: Operations & Logistics: Automate or Die

If you are spending your day doing work that a machine could do, you are not a CEO. You are an overpaid data entry clerk.

There is a final test for every business owner. It isn't a profit margin. It isn't a revenue target. It is a simple, terrifying question: If you left your business for three months today—turned off your phone, went to an island, and did not check your email once—would the business still exist when you came back?

For 95% of service business owners, the answer is No. The business would collapse. The leads wouldn't get answered. The crews wouldn't know where to go. The invoices wouldn't get sent.

If the answer is no, you do not own a business. You own a high-stress job. And the worst part is, you cannot sell a job. You can only sell a system.

In the service industry, Operations is just a fancy word for logistics: getting people to the right place, at the right time, with the right tools, without you having to hold their hand. This chapter is about building the machine that replaces you.

The Darren Protocol: How to Clone Yourself

When I was scaling TWECS (my telecommunications company), I hit a wall. I was flying between Melbourne, Sydney, and Brisbane constantly. I was the bottleneck.

Every decision had to go through me. Every major problem ended up on my desk.

I realized that if one of my Army injuries flared up and I couldn't walk, or if I just burned out, the business stopped. The revenue would hit zero.

I needed a Superintendent. I needed someone who could run the show. I hired a guy named Darren. Darren was a legend —experienced, capable, and hard-working. But hiring him wasn't the solution. Training him to replace me was the solution.

Most founders hire a manager, throw them the keys, and say, Good luck. Then, when the manager fails, the founder takes the keys back and says, Nobody can do it like me. That is ego talking. Here is the exact 3-Phase Handover Process I used with Darren to exit operations.

Phase 1: The Shadow (I Do, You Watch)

For one month, Darren sat in every single meeting with me. He drove to every site visit with me.

The Rule: He was not allowed to speak.

The Goal: He had to watch how I shook hands. He had to watch how I negotiated pricing. He had to see how I handled an angry site manager who was screaming about a delay. He needed to download my brain and my decision-making matrix.

Phase 2: The Handover (You Do, I Watch)

For the next month, we went to the same meetings, but I sat in the corner and said nothing. Darren ran the meeting.

The Rule: I only intervened if he was about to crash the car. If he made a small mistake, I let him make it. We would debrief in the truck afterward. Why did you agree to that timeline? You know we can't hit that.

The Goal: To build his confidence and let the clients see him as the authority.

Phase 3: The Exit (You Do, I Leave)

I stopped going to the meetings. I stopped going to the site. This is the hardest part for a founder. I remember the day a major client called Darren to discuss a contract variation instead of me.

The Ego Hit: A part of me felt hurt. Don't they want to talk to Ron? I built this company!

The Realization: Then I realized I was sitting at home, drinking a coffee, while the business was making money. That phone call to Darren was the sound of freedom.

If you want to scale, you must find your Darren. And you must have the discipline to train him and then get out of his way.

The Audit: Finding What to Automate

You cannot automate a process you don't understand. Before you install any software, you need to audit your own time.

If you don't track your time, you are lying to yourself about how productive you are. You think you are doing high-level strategy, but data will prove you are spending 14 hours a week answering the same three emails.

The Time-Tracking Experiment

For two weeks, I want you to use a simple free tool like Toggl, or even a notepad on your desk. Every time you switch tasks, write it down.

- 08:00 - 08:30: Checking Emails.
- 08:30 - 09:30: Creating Invoices.
- 09:30 - 10:00: Calling crew to see where they are.

At the end of the week, highlight the tasks.

- Green: $1,000/hr work (Sales, Strategy, Partnership negotiation).
- Red: $10/hr work (Data entry, invoicing, scheduling).

The Rule of Repetition: If you do a task once, just do it. If you do a task three times, create a template (SOP). If you do a task five times, automate it.

Here are the specific systems I built to kill the Red tasks.

Tactical Build 1: The Free CRM (Google Forms Strategy)

If you are a small plumber, roofer, or landscaper, do not go out and spend $300 a month on Salesforce or HubSpot. You don't need it yet. Complex software requires complex management. If you don't have a process on paper, software will just make your bad process faster.

I have built a Free CRM using Google Forms that tracks leads, quotes, and revenue. It forces you to capture the right data every time. Here is the SOP.

Step 1: The Input (Google Forms)

Create a new Google Form. This is your Lead Capture tool. You need to set specific fields to force data hygiene.

- Field 1: Full Name.
- Field 2: Service Address (use Google Maps integration if possible).

- Field 3: Service Type (Use a Dropdown Menu: Roof Repair, Full Replacement, Gutter Clean). Do not use a text box here, or your data will be messy.
- Field 4 (The Contractor Hack): File Upload. Label it: Upload photos of the damage.

Why this matters: If a client sends you a photo of a small leak, you know to send the junior guy. If they send a photo of a collapsed roof, you go yourself. You can triage the job from your couch.

Step 2: The Workflow (The On-Site Hack)

Save the link to this form on your phone's home screen.

Scenario: You are on a roof. Your phone rings. It's a new lead.

- Old Way: You scramble for a piece of paper, write down John Smith, 555-0199, stick it in your pocket, wash your pants, and lose the lead.
- New Way: You answer. Hey, I can definitely help. I'm on a roof right now, but I'm going to text you a link. Fill that out, and it will go straight to my dispatch team (even if that team is just you later tonight) to get you a quote.

Step 3: The Pipeline (Google Sheets)

Link the Form to a Google Sheet. This is your database. Add three custom columns to the right of the form data:

Status (Dropdown: New, Quoted, Won, Lost, Invoiced).

Quoted Value ($).

Notes.

Now, every morning, you open the Sheet. You filter by New. You call them. You change the status to Quoted. You have a CRM. It cost $0. It works on any device. It removes the sticky note chaos from your life.

Tactical Build 2: The Medical Clinic (Process Automation)

Automation isn't always about fancy code; sometimes it is about simple communication rules.

I consulted with a medical clinic that was bleeding money.

- The Problem: They had 11 patients a day no-showing.
- The Impact: This pushed the doctors back. Patients in the waiting room got angry. The reception staff spent 3 hours a day calling people asking, Where are you? instead of billing.
- The Founder's Trap: The owner wanted to hire another receptionist to handle the calls. That would have cost $45,000 a year.

The Fix: SMS Automation

We didn't hire anyone. We signed up for a simple SMS reminder service (like Twilio or a plugin for their booking software). We set up a specific cadence:

24 Hours Prior: Hi [Name], your appointment with Dr. Smith is tomorrow at 2PM. Reply Y to confirm.

2 Hours Prior: Hi [Name], see you in 2 hours. Here is the Google Maps link for parking.

The Result: No-shows dropped from 11 per day to 3 per day. We recovered 8 billable appointments per day. We recovered 15 hours of staff wages per week because they weren't chasing people. The system cost $50 a month. The staff member would have cost $3,500 a month. This is how you replace labor with logic.

Tactical Build 3: The Dispatch App (Stop the Phone Tag)

If you run a field service business (electricians, cleaners, pest control), the Phone Tag game is killing your efficiency.

The Old Way: You get a job. You call Tech A. He doesn't answer because he's driving. You call Tech B. He answers but says he doesn't have the parts. You call Tech A again. You text him the address. He texts back Can't find it. You are the router. You are the bottleneck.

The New Way: Asynchronous Dispatch

You need to move to a Dispatch App (like ServiceM8 or Housecall Pro). If you are on a budget, you can build a light version using Trello or Monday.com.

When a job comes in via your Google Form (from Build 1), it goes onto a board. You assign it to Tech A.

- The Notification: Tech A's phone pings. He sees the address, the photos of the damage (from the client), and the required parts.
- The Action: He clicks Accept. You see the status change on your dashboard.
- The Result: Zero phone calls made. You didn't break your focus. He didn't have to pull over the van to write down an address.

By removing the need for a conversation, you speed up the velocity of the entire company.

Tactical Build 4: The Python Script (Admin Heavy Lifting)

Sometimes, you have a task that is so massive, a human shouldn't do it at all.

The Scenario: I once had a project where we needed to process 30,000 lines of data. It was home address data that needed to be sorted by zip code, formatted, and checked against a Do Not Call list.

- Manual Estimate: I calculated that if I put an admin staff member on this, it would take them 2 weeks of full-time work (80 hours). At $25/hour, that's a $2,000 cost, plus the risk of human error (which is 100% guaranteed with that much data).

The Automation: I am not a coder. But I know what code can do. I went to a freelancer site (Upwork) and found a Python developer. I said: Here is a CSV file. I need a script that sorts Column A by Zip Code, removes duplicates, and deletes any row that matches this 'Do Not Call' list.

The Cost: The developer charged me $50. He sent me the script. I ran it on my computer. It finished the job in 45 seconds.

The Lesson: 2 weeks of work vs. 45 seconds. $2,000 vs. $50. You do not need to learn Python. You just need to realize that data processing is not a human job. If you find yourself staring at Excel for more than an hour, you are wasting your life. Hire a script writer to automate it once, and run it forever.

Tactical Build 5: The AI Email Reader (The Time Saver)

Let's look at a micro-automation that saves you 30 minutes a day. As a founder, your inbox is a warzone. You get 100+ emails a day. Reading them all takes an hour.

The Solution: I use an AI agent (you can set this up with tools like Zapier connecting Gmail to OpenAI).

- The Trigger: When a new email arrives that is longer than 200 words.
- The Action: The AI reads the email and summarizes it into three bullet points.

Sender Intent: (e.g., They want a refund).

Key Details: (e.g., Invoice #404, Job on Main St).

Suggested Action: (e.g., Forward to Accounts).

- The Delivery: It sends me this summary on Slack or puts it at the top of the email.

The Math: This saves me about 1 minute per email. 30 emails a day = 30 minutes saved. 30 minutes x 5 days = 2.5 hours a week. 2.5 hours x 52 weeks = 130 hours a year.

That is three full weeks of work (or holiday) that I have reclaimed just by having a robot read my emails.

Summary: The System is the Product

You need to shift your identity. You are not a Roofer. You are a Builder of Roofing Systems. You are not a Doctor. You are an Architect of Medical Processes.

Every time you answer a question, ask yourself: How can I document this so I never have to answer it again? Every time you fix a problem, ask yourself: What checklist was missing that allowed this to happen?

Clone Yourself: Use the Darren Protocol (Shadow, Handover, Exit).

Audit Your Time: Find the repetitive tasks.

Build the Free CRM: Stop losing leads on sticky notes.

Automate Communication: Use SMS and Dispatch apps to stop the phone tag.

Use Code: Spend $50 on a script to save $2,000 in labor.

If you do this, you will eventually reach the point where you can turn off your phone, fly to that island, and come back to a bank account that is bigger than when you left. That is the definition of winning the war.

KEY TAKEAWAYS

✓ If you're doing the same task 3+ times, automate it

✓ Standard Operating Procedures (SOPs) let you scale without chaos

✓ Use AI tools for admin, scheduling, and customer communication

✓ Your job is to work ON the business, not just IN it

✓ Systems create freedom—chaos creates burnout

CHAPTER 7: The Commander's Log: Tracking, Accountability & The Science of Self-Reflection

You have built the lead engine. You have hired the team. You have automated the operations. The external machine is running.

But there is one failure point left that can destroy everything: You.

The external business is only as strong as the internal operator. If you, the Commander, are exhausted, unfocused, or lying to yourself about your progress, the troops will falter, and the mission will fail.

Most business owners think tracking means looking at a Profit & Loss statement once a month. That is not tracking; that is an autopsy. That tells you what died last month. It does not tell you why it died, or how to keep it alive today.

I have found that 92% of people abandon their goals within two weeks. They don't fail because they are lazy. They don't fail because they lack vision. They fail because they are tracking it wrong. They treat goals as wishes rather than systems.

This chapter is about The Commander's Log. It is about the brutal, unglamorous work of self-reflection. It is about turning your feelings into data, so you can pivot your business before you hit the iceberg.

The Mirror Test: Why You Must Document to Survive

Why do you need to write things down? Why do you need a Digital Diary? Because the human brain is designed to protect your ego.

If you have a bad week—you missed your sales calls, you ate garbage food, you snapped at your employees—your brain will delete that memory to protect your self-esteem. You will look back at the month and say, I worked hard. The market is just tough right now.

That is a lie.

If you track your data daily, the spreadsheet doesn't lie. The spreadsheet says: You worked hard on Tuesday. But on Wednesday, Thursday, and Friday, you slept 5 hours, your focus score was a 3/10, and you completed 0% of your revenue-generating tasks.

You cannot pivot a business structure, a process, or a system based on a feeling. You can only pivot based on quantifiable facts.

- Without Tracking: I feel like we aren't closing deals. Maybe the leads are bad? (You fire the marketing agency).
- With Tracking: The data shows I only followed up with 20% of leads this week because I was tired. (You fix your sleep schedule, keep the agency, and make money).

Self-reflection is not about crying in a journal. It is a tactical debrief. In the Army, after every operation, we did an After Action Review (AAR). What happened? Why did it happen? How do we fix it? You must do the same for your life.

Tool 1: The S.M.A.R.T. Goal Breakdown (Turning Visions into Math)

Most people set goals like this: I want to open my own clinic. or I want to get more leads.

These are not goals. These are dreams. And dreams do not pay the rent.

You must turn these vague desires into Mathematics. You must use the S.M.A.R.T. framework: Specific, Measurable, Achievable, Relevant, Time-Bound.

Let me walk you through two real-world examples of how I force my clients to break down a vision into a 90-day execution plan using my Free SMART Goals Template.

Example A: The 12-Month Vision (Dr. Sarah)

Let's look at Dr. Sarah, a chiropractor making $80,000 a year as an associate. Her vision is: I want to start my own clinic. That is too big. It's overwhelming. We need to break it down into numbers.

The Objective: Launch a private clinic within 12 months that generates $10,000 in Monthly Recurring Revenue (MRR). To hit $10k MRR, she needs 50 active patients paying an average of $200/month.

Now, we break this down into quarterly sprints:

Quarter 1 (The Foundation):

- Goal: Secure commercial lease and complete office build-out.
- Measurable: Signed lease document by Month 1. Equipment installation 100% complete by Month 3.
- Budget: $50,000 allocated for build-out.

- The Tracker: In the template, she marks this as In Progress. If by week 6 she hasn't signed a lease, the data screams at her. She is behind. She must pivot her search strategy immediately.

Quarter 4 (The Growth Phase):

- Goal: Reach 50 active patients.
- Measurable: 15 new patient inquiries per week. 20% conversion rate.
- The Action: If she is only getting 5 inquiries, she knows the problem is Marketing. If she is getting 20 inquiries but only signing 2 patients, she knows the problem is Sales.

By breaking Open a Clinic down into 15 inquiries per week, she has a number she can track every single day.

Example B: The 90-Day Sprint (Mike the Remodeler)

Mike is a bathroom remodeler. His goal: I want more work. We need to tighten that.

The Objective: Generate 30 qualified leads in the next 90 days specifically through Google Business Profile optimization.

The Measurables (The Math):

Reviews: Go from 8 reviews to 25 five-star reviews.

Traffic: Increase website visitors from 200 to 500 per month.

Revenue: Close 20% of the 30 leads (6 jobs). Average job $8,000. Total Revenue Target: $48,000.

How Mike Tracks This: Every Friday, Mike looks at his dashboard.

- Week 1: I got 0 new reviews.
- Self-Reflection: Why? I forgot to ask.
- Pivot: Next week, I will print the QR code card (from Chapter 4) and hand it to every client.
- Week 2: I got 3 reviews.

Because he tracked the number, he identified the failure (forgetting to ask), implemented a system (the QR code), and saw the result. If he wasn't tracking, he would just say, Google doesn't work.

Tool 2: The Digital Diary (The 90-Day System)

Now that you have the math, you need the daily discipline to execute it. I have built a Digital Diary tool that tracks your performance. This is not a Dear Diary book. This is a spreadsheet that tracks your Energy, Mood, Focus, and Habits.

You cannot manage what you do not measure.

The Non-Negotiables (Habit Tracking)

In the Setup tab of the diary, you define your Daily Actions. These are the small, boring things that lead to the big result.

- For Dr. Sarah: Call 5 local businesses for referral partnerships.
- For Mike: Ask every client for a review.
- For You: Maybe it's Send 10 cold emails or Check cash flow.

The Golden Rule: The Pattern

I have a principle in my diary that I want you to burn into your brain: Missing one day is an accident. Missing two days is a pattern.

If you miss your daily action on Tuesday, fine. You are human. If you miss it on Wednesday, you are now forming a new habit: the habit of failure. The Digital Diary visualizes this. You see a row of Green (Success) followed by two days of Red (Failure). That visual feedback is painful. It forces you to self-reflect: Why am I slipping? Am I lazy, or is the goal unrealistic?

Correlation Tracking: The Sleep = Revenue Equation

This is the most powerful feature of the tool, and it proves that your personal biology dictates your business success.

The Digital Diary tracks your Sleep and your Focus on a scale of 1-10. It then calculates a Correlation Score.

The Scenario: You might think you can hustle on 4 hours of sleep. You think you are grinding. But after 30 days, the data will show you a correlation score of 1.0 (Perfect Correlation).

- The Data: On days you slept 5 hours, your Focus score was 3/10. On days your Focus was 3/10, your Habit Completion (Sales calls) was 0%.
- The Conclusion: Lack of sleep is directly costing you revenue.

You are not hustling; you are sabotaging your bank account. When you see this data, self-reflection becomes easy.

- Question: Why are my sales down?
- Answer: Because I am staying up until 2 AM watching Netflix, which kills my focus, which makes me avoid the phone.

- The Pivot: Go to bed at 10 PM.

This is data-driven personal performance. You stop guessing why you are failing and start seeing the mathematical root cause.

The Interrogation: Questions for Self-Reflection

You need to schedule a meeting with yourself. I recommend doing this Weekly (Sunday night or Monday morning). Open your tracker. Look at the Red and Green cells. Then, ask yourself these hard questions. Do not bullshit the answers.

The Tactical Questions

Did I hit my non-negotiables this week? (Yes/No). If No, was it a lack of time, or a lack of discipline? Be honest.

What drained my energy this week? Was it a specific client? A specific employee? If a client drains you every week, fire them. If an employee drains you, train them or fire them.

What was the One Thing that actually moved the needle? We often confuse being busy with being productive. Did you spend 4 hours on email (busy work) and 0 hours on sales (productive work)?

Am I closer to the 90-day vision than I was last week? If the answer is no, you are stagnant. Stagnation in business is death.

The Strategic Questions (The Pivot)

Is the goal still relevant? Sometimes we set a goal (e.g., Post on TikTok daily) and realize after 3 weeks it brings zero revenue. The Pivot: Stop doing it. Redirect that energy to cold calling.

Where am I the bottleneck? Look at your Not Done tasks. Are they not done because you have to do them? The Pivot: Delegate. Create an SOP. Use the delegation strategies from Chapter 6.

If I repeat this week's performance for the next year, will I be rich or broke? This is the ultimate reality check.

Case Study: The Pivot in Action

Let me tell you about a client, a hydraulics company owner (Mr. Hose). He had a goal: Increase revenue. Vague. Useless. We implemented the tracking.

- The Data: We tracked his Lead Response Time. We found that his team was taking 4 hours to call back leads.
- The Reflection: Why? Because they were busy fixing hoses in the shop.
- The Pivot: We changed the system. The phone now routed to a dedicated person, not the guys on the tools.
- The Result: Response time dropped to 5 minutes. Revenue increased by $51,000 in two months.

This result did not come from working harder. It came from tracking a number, reflecting on why it was bad, and pivoting the system.

Summary: The Commander's Discipline

You are the Commander of your life and your business. A Commander does not guess. A Commander looks at the map, checks the supply lines, and evaluates the morale of the troops.

Break it Down: Use the SMART Goals Template to turn I want to be rich into I need 20 leads a month.

Track Daily: Use the Digital Diary. Track your sleep, your mood, and your non-negotiables.

Spot the Pattern: Missing once is an accident. Missing twice is a pattern. Kill the pattern before it kills your business.

Interrogate Yourself: Every Sunday, ask the hard questions. If something isn't working, Pivot. Do not stay the course just because you said you would.

You have the tools. You have the templates. Now, you need the discipline to fill them out every single day. If you do this, you will look back in 90 days and you won't recognize your life.

KEY TAKEAWAYS

✓ What gets measured gets managed—track your numbers weekly

✓ Ask yourself: 'If I repeat this week for a year, will I be rich or broke?'

✓ Review leads, conversions, revenue, and profit every single week

✓ Accountability partners or coaches accelerate your progress

✓ The best operators are obsessed with their data

CHAPTER 8: Future-Proofing: AI, Inflation & The Exit

You might be winning the battle today. You might have cash flow, a good team, and leads coming in. But are you ready for the war that is coming tomorrow?

We are living in unprecedented times. I look at the financial systems of the world—the printing of money, the interest rates, the technological shifts—and I see a storm coming. But the biggest storm isn't inflation, and it isn't a recession. It is Artificial Intelligence.

I have been screaming this from the rooftops for years: AI is coming for your business. If you are a young bloke, or even an old dog in business, my advice is simple: Get off your ass and learn as much about AI as you humanly possibly can.

If you sit down at a computer for the majority of your work, you are in trouble. In the next couple of years, your job could be replaced. Your business could be replaced. If you are a service business owner and you do not start looking to use AI across your systems, your lead management, and your client relationships, you are in for a world of hurt.

This chapter is about Future-Proofing. It is about building a business that is leaner, faster, and more lethal than the competition. It is about understanding what robots can do, what they can't do, and how to position yourself to sell your business for millions instead of closing the doors for pennies.

The AI Wave: Adapt or Die

Let's be brutally honest. The era of the bloated office staff is over. I have built multi-million dollar companies with 30 employees. I know the headache of managing large teams. Today, leaner and faster organizations that adapt quickly are the ones that are going to win this game.

The Computer Job Reality Check

If your value to the marketplace involves typing on a keyboard, processing data, or answering basic emails, you are on a clock. Marketing jobs, especially at the junior level, are shrinking. Administrative roles are vanishing. Why? Because an AI agent can read 1,000 emails, categorize them, draft responses, and update the CRM in seconds for pennies.

The Dirty Jobs Safety Net

However, if you are in the trades—if you are a plumber, a roofer, an electrician, or a landscaper—you are safe from the robots for a long time. I predict that humanoid robots will take over the logistics industry first.

The Logic: Teaching a robot to pick up a standardized box from a standardized shelf and move it to a standardized truck is programmable. It is repetitive.

The Trade Reality: Teaching a robot to climb into a hot attic, navigate around unique ductwork, identify a specific leak in a copper pipe, and solder it while balancing on a joist? That is incredibly difficult. No two houses are the same.

If you own a trade business, your value is about to skyrocket. As white-collar jobs get eaten by AI, the dirty jobs will become the wealthy jobs. But you must use AI to run the office side of that business, or you will be outcompeted on speed and price.

Tactical Guide: Replacing Humans with AI (My Personal Case Studies)

I don't just preach this; I do it. I have replaced entire departments with AI systems. Here is how I am using it right now to remain up-to-date and profitable.

Example 1: The Link Building Replacement

In the SEO world, building backlinks (getting other sites to link to you) is tedious and expensive. You used to have to hire an agency or a dedicated staff member to hunt for sites, email them, and negotiate.

- The Old Way: Pay an agency $2,000 a month. They send generic emails. They get low results.
- The AI Way: I built a system where I feed a spreadsheet of keywords into an AI. It scrapes the web for relevant sites. It analyzes the URL to see if it's a good fit. It drafts a personalized outreach email based on the content of that specific site.
- The Result: I don't need to hire a link-building agency ever again. I can do the work of three people in one afternoon.

Example 2: The Content Machine

I track my freelancers not by hours, but by output. If I hire a writer, I know that with AI assistance, they should be able to produce four to five high-quality blog posts a day. If they bill me for 8 hours and produce two blogs, I know they aren't using the tools. I can replace them with someone who does. This sounds harsh, but business is about efficiency. If you are not using AI to 10x your output, you are stealing from your own profit margin.

Tactical Tool: The Competitor Spy (SWOT Analysis Agent)

You cannot win a war if you don't know who you are fighting. Most business owners guess at what their competitors are doing. I use AI to know.

I built a specific tool called the Google Maps Review Analyzer. This tool uses AI to scrape your competitors' public reviews and perform a SWOT Analysis (Strengths, Weaknesses, Opportunities, Threats) in seconds.

Why Reviews?

Reviews are the source of truth. Your competitor's marketing says they are The Best. Their reviews say, They never answer the phone, or They overcharged me. That gap is where you make your money.

The Workflow (Step-by-Step)

The Reconnaissance: Go to Google Maps. Find your top three competitors. Copy the URL of their business profile.

The Extraction: Paste those URLs into my free Review Analyzer tool (available at ronaldosborne.org).

The AI Analysis: The tool scrapes the reviews and feeds them into an AI model (like Claude or OpenAI). It doesn't just read them; it analyzes the sentiment.

The Output: It gives you a breakdown like this:

- Weakness: Competitor X has great workmanship, but 40% of reviews complain about billing transparency and surprise fees.

- Threat: Heavy reliance on one key employee (e.g., 'Mike is great'). If Mike leaves, the business fails.

The Strategic Pivot: Once you see that your competitor is hated for Billing Surprises, you launch a marketing campaign: City Roofing – The No-Surprise Price Guarantee. You win the market not by being better at roofing, but by attacking their specific weakness. You couldn't do this analysis manually without reading 500 reviews. AI does it in 30 seconds.

The Human Moat: What AI Cannot Replace

If AI can write emails, schedule appointments, and analyze data, what is left for you?

Connection.

The best way you can protect yourself is by offering something that AI cannot replace: Trust and Face-to-Face Relationships.

The Steve Smith Effect

There is a famous Australian cricketer named Steve Smith. He launched an oat milk company. But if you look at his Instagram, he barely promotes it (before it was sold). He keeps his brand off to the side. That is a mistake in my opinion. In the AI era, faceless brands will die. People want to buy from people. If I pick up the phone and call a business, and I speak to an AI, it's efficient. But if I speak to the founder, or if I see a video of the founder explaining the process, trust skyrockets.

Strategy: The Hot Lunch (B2B)

This is why I advocate for the Hot Lunch strategy for B2B sales. You can send 1,000 AI-generated emails. Or, you can call a Real Estate Agent and say, I want to buy you lunch. AI cannot eat lunch. AI cannot shake a hand. AI cannot look a man in the eye and give him your word. Double down on the human element. Use AI to handle the admin so you can spend 90% of your time shaking hands and building trust.

The Exit: Founder vs. System

You are building this business to give you freedom. But you will never have freedom if the business is you.

There is a final test for every business owner. It isn't a profit margin. It is a simple question: If you left your business for three months today, would it still exist when you came back?

If the answer is no, you don't own a business. You own a high-stress job. And you cannot sell a job.

Valuation: The Ronald Osborne Problem

I often advise people on buying and selling businesses. Do NOT buy a business where the founder is the brand.

- Case A: Ronald Osborne Coaching. This business relies on me. If I sell it, the new owner buys my name. If I leave, the value drops to zero. It is very hard to sell this business because it is dependent on my face and my voice.
- Case B: The T-Shirt Store / The Franchise. If you run a laundromat or a roofing company named City Roofing with SOPs, the buyer is buying a machine. They put $1 in, they get $2 out. It doesn't matter who unlocks the door.

If you want to exit for millions, you must build City Plumbing, not Mike's Plumbing. You need documented processes so that any technician can step into the van and do the job exactly how you would. You need to hire a Darren (like I did with my superintendent) to replace you in the field so you can focus on the asset.

KEY TAKEAWAYS

✓ AI is not coming—it's here. Adapt or become irrelevant

✓ Build your business to be sellable, even if you never sell

✓ Recurring revenue and documented systems increase business value

✓ Inflation and economic shifts reward those with cash reserves

✓ Your exit strategy should be planned from day one

CONCLUSION: The Crying on the Couch Story

We have covered the tactics. We have covered the tools. We have covered the AI revolution.

But before we part ways, I need to have a serious conversation with you about the cost of this life.

Business is the hardest thing I have ever done. I was a soldier in the Australian Army. I served with good men. I slept in the mud. I pushed my body to the limit until I was medically discharged. And I will tell you the honest truth: I have had far more sleepless nights as a business owner than I ever did as a soldier.

In the Army, you have a brotherhood. You have orders. Even when it sucks, you know what you have to do. In business, you are alone. If the payroll doesn't clear, it's on you. If the client sues, it's on you. If the market crashes, it's on you.

The Moment of Truth

I remember vividly the moment I realized the toll it had taken. I had built the multi-million dollar company. I had the cars. I had the status. I had made it by every metric society gave me. I was able to retire by the time I was 30.

And I remember sitting on the couch in my apartment, completely alone, and tears in my eyes.

I wasn't crying tears of joy. I was upset because I was exhausted. I had sacrificed relationships. I had missed family events. I had worked 12-hour days, 7 days a week, for years.

I realized that money without a life is just a different kind of prison.

Why I Tell You This

I tell you this not to scare you, but to prepare you. If you are doing this just for the money, go get a job. Go get a high-paying sales job. You can make $200,000 a year, and when you clock off at 5 PM, you can turn your phone off. You can relax. As a business owner, you can never turn your phone off. Your business is your baby. It screams in the middle of the night.

You need to be sure that this is what you want. You need to be sure that the freedom you are fighting for is worth the sacrifice you are making today.

Your Marching Orders

If you are sure—if you have the grit, the will, and the discipline—then you have everything you need in this manual.

Validate your idea. Don't chase pipe dreams.

Protect your cash flow. Do not go into debt for things that don't pay you back.

Automate everything. Use the AI tools I gave you.

Hire for loyalty. Treat your team like family, but set boundaries.

Build a system, not a job. Make yourself redundant.

I have given you the map. I have given you the tools. The free templates, the scrapers, the calculators—they are all there on ronaldosborne.org.

The rest is up to you. Opportunity waits for no man.

Now, get to work.

Author's Note

If you have read this book and you realize that your business has holes in it—if you are bleeding cash, struggling to hire, or terrified of AI—do not fight this war alone. I offer a Free 15-Minute Discovery Call. This isn't a sales pitch. It is a diagnosis. We will look at your business, identify the bottleneck, and I will point you in the right direction.

If you are doing over $150,000 a year, I also offer a revenue audit where I guarantee that I will find at least $10,000 in additional revenue for your business, or if I don't, I'll pay you $100 for wasting your time.

Reach out to me. Let's fix your organization.

Book your call at ronaldosborne.org.

About the Author

Ronald Osborne is an award-winning international business coach who has helped thousands of service businesses around the world improve their organisations and scale to new heights.

A proud Australian Army veteran, Ronald brings military discipline and strategic thinking to the business world. After his service, he built TWECS (Telecommunications Wireless Electrical Civil Construction Solutions) from a startup to a $5.7 million operation with over 30 employees operating across Australia's east coast.

Ronald holds an MBA specialising in finance and has founded multiple successful companies spanning construction, digital marketing, and business coaching. His no-nonsense approach combines real-world experience with data-driven strategies that actually work.

Today, Ronald helps local service business owners escape the trap of being "self-employed labourers" and build systems that generate wealth and freedom.

Get all the free tools, templates, and resources mentioned in this book:

ronaldosborne.org

KEY TAKEAWAYS

✓ Every successful operator has cried on the couch—you're not alone

✓ The gap between where you are and where you want to be is just work

✓ Execution beats strategy every time—stop planning, start doing

✓ Get support at ronaldosborne.org—free tools, templates, and coaching

WORKSHEETS

Practical tools to implement what you've learned

WORKSHEET: The Homeless Test

Calculate Your True Risk Tolerance

Step 1: Calculate Your Monthly Survival Number

What is the absolute minimum you need each month to keep a roof over your head and food on the table? Be ruthless—no luxuries.

Rent/Mortgage: $ ____________
Utilities: $ ____________
Food (basic): $ ____________
Transport: $ ____________
Insurance: $ ____________
Phone/Internet: $ ____________
Other essentials: $ ____________

TOTAL MONTHLY SURVIVAL NUMBER: $______________

Step 2: Calculate Your Runway

Current Savings: $ ____________
Assets you could sell: $ ____________
TOTAL AVAILABLE: $ ____________

YOUR RUNWAY = Total Available ÷ Survival Number = _________ months

Step 3: The Decision

If your runway is less than 6 months: Start as a side hustle—don't quit your job yet.

If your runway is 6-12 months: You can take calculated risks with a solid plan.

If your runway is 12+ months: You have room to go all-in.

My decision:

WORKSHEET: Break-Even Analysis

Know Your Numbers Before You Spend a Dollar on Marketing

Step 1: Fixed Costs (Monthly)

Rent/Office: $ ____________

Salaries (including yours): $ ____________

Software/Subscriptions: $ ____________

Insurance: $ ____________

Vehicle costs: $ ____________

Other fixed costs: $ ____________

TOTAL FIXED COSTS: $____________

Step 2: Variable Costs Per Job

Materials per job: $ ____________

Labour per job: $ ____________

Other variable costs: $ ____________

TOTAL VARIABLE COST PER JOB: $____________

Step 3: Calculate Break-Even

Average job price: $ ____________

Contribution Margin = Job Price − Variable Cost = $____________

Break-Even Point = Fixed Costs ÷ Contribution Margin = ________ jobs/month

This means you need to complete at least this many jobs each month just to cover your costs. Everything above this number is profit.

WORKSHEET: Weekly Operator Reflection

The Science of Self-Reflection

Week of: ____________________

The Critical Question:

If I repeat this week's performance for the next year, will I be rich or broke?

This Week's Numbers:

Revenue: $ ____________________
Jobs completed: ____________________
New leads generated: ____________________
Quotes sent: ____________________
Conversion rate: ____________________

What worked well this week?

What didn't work? What needs to change?

One action I commit to taking next week:

WORKSHEET: Weekly Operator Reflection

Week 2

Week of: ____________________

The Critical Question:

If I repeat this week's performance for the next year, will I be rich or broke?

This Week's Numbers:

Revenue: $ ____________________
Jobs completed: ____________________
New leads generated: ____________________
Quotes sent: ____________________
Conversion rate: ____________________

What worked well this week?

What didn't work? What needs to change?

One action I commit to taking next week:

WORKSHEET: Weekly Operator Reflection

Week 3

Week of: ____________________

The Critical Question:

If I repeat this week's performance for the next year, will I be rich or broke?

This Week's Numbers:

Revenue: $

Jobs completed:

New leads generated:

Quotes sent:

Conversion rate:

What worked well this week?

What didn't work? What needs to change?

One action I commit to taking next week:

WORKSHEET: Weekly Operator Reflection

Week 4

Week of: ____________________

The Critical Question:

If I repeat this week's performance for the next year, will I be rich or broke?

This Week's Numbers:

Revenue: $ ____________________
Jobs completed: ____________________
New leads generated: ____________________
Quotes sent: ____________________
Conversion rate: ____________________

What worked well this week?

What didn't work? What needs to change?

One action I commit to taking next week:

RESOURCES

Free tools, templates, and ways to connect

Free Business Tools & Templates

Access my complete collection of business tools, spreadsheets, and calculators worth over $15,000—completely free:

goto.ronaldosborne.org/Ronald_Osborne_Business_Success_Cheat_Sheets

Book a Discovery Call

Ready to take your service business to the next level? Book a free discovery call to discuss your specific situation:

goto.ronaldosborne.org/Book_Ronald_Osborne

Connect With Me

YouTube: **youtube.com/@ronaldosbornebusinesscoach**

X (Twitter): **x.com/Ronaldosbornebc**

Facebook: **facebook.com/RonaldOsbornebusinesscoach**

LinkedIn: **linkedin.com/in/ronaldosborne-osbornedigitalmarketing**

Website: **ronaldosborne.org**

ABOUT THE AUTHOR

Ronald Osborne is an award-winning international business coach, Australian Army veteran, and founder of multiple successful businesses.

He built TWECS, a telecommunications company, from zero to $5.7 million in revenue with over 30 employees operating across Australia's east coast.

With an MBA specializing in finance and real-world experience scaling service businesses across Australia, America, and the UAE, Ronald now coaches local service business owners to build profitable, scalable operations.

He lives by a simple philosophy: lead with value. That's why you'll find thousands of dollars worth of free tools, templates, and resources on his website.

ronaldosborne.org

NOTES

NOTES

NOTES

NOTES

NOTES

NOTES

NOTES

NOTES

NOTES

NOTES

NOTES

NOTES

NOTES

NOTES

NOTES

NOTES

NOTES

NOTES

NOTES

NOTES

NOTES

NOTES

NOTES

NOTES

Made in United States
Cleveland, OH
05 November 2026

47669896R00070